The Song in My Night

Hilda Harder

Hilda Harder

Produced by:

FriesenPress

Suite 300 – 852 Fort Street
Victoria, BC, Canada V8W 1H8

www.friesenpress.com

Distributed to the trade by The Ingram Book Company

Lovingly dedicated to my family.

The Song in My Night

*"… I went down to the potter's house, and, behold,
he wrought a work on the wheels. And the vessel that he
made of clay was marred in the hand of the potter…"*
Jeremiah 18:3–4, KJV

I was born, in 1928, with congenitally dislocated hips. This is my story as I journeyed through life at a slower pace.

Fraser River, Mission, BC
Made in Canada by the Gowen, Sutton Co Ltd, Vancouver, BC

I grew up on a farm in the peaceful Fraser Valley in southern British Columbia. I had a brother and a mother, but most of all I had a dad.

Ours was a plain house, with square high-ceilinged rooms and a large unfinished attic. Dad planted apple, pear, and plum trees on the blizzard side where the wind swept across the flats from the river in winter. On the south side, was his garden of vegetables, currant and gooseberry bushes, and towering above all was a Bing cherry tree.

Across the field and over the tracks, lived Uncle
Bert, my mother's oldest brother, the boss man of the
clan. Next door lived Grandma and Grandpa.

My grandma
full of love
   and kindly
   a beautiful lady
even at eighty.
Elegant
with a serenity born of trials
by my grandfather's wiles;
   he drank too much too often.

She took abuse
with accustomed calm
   her touch, her look,
a healing balm.

My grandma was a special sort
   to wipe a tear
   and soothe a heart.

She got cancer
   that lovely lady
   full of grace—
gentle hands
upon my face.

I wish I'd known her better;
My grandma died when I was ten.

Grandma Farr
Collection of Family Photographs

My young life was spent mostly with my
daddy, in between stays at the hospital.

"It's a game, you see. Can you count
with me? Ten ..." said a voice.

"Ten," I answered.

They placed an evil-smelling cloth over my nose. "Nine."

"Nine," I answered, and fought with
all my three-year-old strength.

"Eight."

"Eight," I slurred, battling the whirlwind that grabbed me…

"Seven."

…but I was lost in its roaring sickening centre.

I woke up in casts, nauseated, and in pain. *Oh Daddy, where are you?* I didn't know that it broke his tender heart and that he had suffered a massive heart attack. Eventually we both healed and were home again.

I followed him like a shadow…

My daddy was a little man
born of Adam's race;
loving trust I felt for him
as I looked upon his face.

I felt special
    protected by family and friends
but most of all
in the loving arms
of my father.

A veteran of the First World War, Dad's heart and lungs were damaged by mustard gas at Vimy Ridge.

John Clarke Sanders
Photographer Unknown

We survived on his small pension and big garden, the fruit trees, milk from our Jersey cow, chickens and eggs. We never knew that we were poor. Dad would take me with him to the barn to do the chores. Together we'd coax a newborn calf to drink its first warm milk—its rasping tongue, sucking milk from between my fingers, gave me shivers of delight. We'd check the eggs, and I'd listen to the pecking from within until each wet chick emerged.

Dad would milk the cow, and I would pet the baby things. He'd hold my hand as we walked back to the house.

We would look up into the fathomless skies to find the Big Dipper, before becoming lost in the wonder of the Milky Way. I knew that there was a God watching, waiting...

I'd tighten my grip
on Daddy's warm hand
    as the blackness of darkness
stole over the land;
    as the trees rustled
their leaves in flight
    the stars shone distant
in the clear cold night.

We would sit in the evenings close to the fireplace. The flames leapt and chased the air, bringing faraway thoughts of faraway places.

The Sanders Home, Odell, England
Collection of Family Photographs

The River Ouse, Odell, England
Photographer Unknown

Daddy would tell us about his childhood in England…

I can almost hear him now
    telling half-truths made beautiful
by the poetry in his soul:
    The old stone house
with window ledges
large enough
for a boy to sit upon.
    Ivy climbing up the walls
    The hedge with its hidey holes
    The fireplace
with a spit,
    And the headmaster
with a cane.

Sometimes, in a pensive mood, he
would tell us about the war.

"Why the killing?
Why the wanton waste of life?"
    How many children would hold out arms
for fathers who would never come home again?
    How many wives would smother sobs
within lonely pillows?

Parents died a little
as bone of their bone
and flesh of their flesh
lay rotting
    black and bloated
    in the sun.

Why are we caught
 in this cage of hate?
   "Water, please mate!"
one would rasp through blistered lips.
   "Write a letter for me?" begged another.

He slept
    when he slept
in the filth and muck of the trench.
He caught lice.
He didn't notice what he ate
    or if he ate.
A tale of terror
told in his tender eyes.

John Clarke Sanders
Photographer Unknown

Cold fear clutched me on my first day of
school. Bereft of the comforting cocoon of
family love, I faced the fact; I was different.

A ladybug crawled along my arm
while I sat upon
the bottom step
    alone
and feigned great interest
in its progress.

Children ran and jumped
and laughed.
I held tight to the rail;
put my best foot forward
and pulled myself
behind.

The ladybug flew away.

They wouldn't walk with me
and so I walked alone.
They snickered
    and they mocked me
for I had a crippled bone.

Together, Daddy and I took a runty piglet, wrapped it in flannel, and cozied it in a box behind the old cookstove. We bottle fed it with sweet warm milk, scratched its ears and belly, and watched it thrive. It grew and followed at our heels. I also grew, and as I grew, I questioned...

"Why me, God?
Why the path of pain.
Do you hear my cry?
Are you there, God?"

Hilda Sanders (1942)
Collection of Family Photographs

In the summer we'd gather
with friends and neighbours
    berry pickers
and cousins
who loved to come.

We didn't have a car
and so we walked
    picnicking
by the cool waterfall
at the base of the mountain
    swimming at Pages Lake
    picking blackberries
and wild hazelnuts.

After berry-picking season
we had holidays at Birch Bay
    boiling fresh-caught crab
Or we'd rent a room for a week
near Stanley Park …
and Woodwards or
the White Lunch.

White Lunch Ltd., Granville Street, Vancouver, BC
Credits: "City of Vancouver Archives"
Reference Code: AM1535-:CVA995167
Photographer: Thompson, Stuart

Woodwards Department Store, Vancouver, BC
Credits: "City of Vancouver Archives" Reference Code: AM1184-S3-:CVA1184-1337
Photographer: Lindsay, Jack

The train brought men
in the thirties
   hungry men
never turned away
but given a meal
and a bed of straw.

   No smoking in the barn
was the only rule.

An old peddler
   pushing his wheelbarrow display
of needles
threads and such
always ended his day
with us.

A vaudeville family
   down on their luck
entertained us
with song and dance
   all met
with happy acceptance.

My younger days were fondly remembered with my family. We'd sleep on the front porch in summer. Harry and cousin Bill at one end and me at the other. I'd wake to survey my world with happy anticipation. Honeysuckles wafted a sweet scent in the morning mist, its vines a-green about me. I opened my eyes to Dad's labour of love, a large expanse of lawn with three circles of flowers bordered with rocks, painted white. The lawn was edged with a row of laburnum trees, dripping yellow blossoms, their branches touching each other, like angels holding protecting arms to shelter this little Eden. Two stately cedar trees stood as sentinels guarding their own. In this deep dark corner, he made a bench from barrel staves. Here he planted the flower of his choice, the lily-of-the-valley. It was my secret place, where I'd sit and quietly conclude, "This must be the most beautiful place in the whole world!" but for me the centre of it all was my dad.

He taught me little things
like not to speak while fishing;
    to hear the gentle hum of bees
and flies and things
    wind sifting softly through the trees
the swirling living river
and birds
    to see cotton clouds crawling
trailing tendrils across the sky
    odd markings on a leaf
    and a beetle on a branch.

Taking his army knapsack, he'd put in sandwiches and
a thermos of tea and methodically fit it on his shoulders.
We'd walk the railway tracks and across the trestle.

Far below
white water
dashed over rocks
in its last glad song
to join the river
    and be lost in its many waters.
Blackberry brambles
    reached their thorny grasps.
Squirrels
    scolded us with lively chatter.
Lady slippers
    hid close to the black earth.

Dad would throw out his line and prop his rod against a
forked stick, high on the bank. An old cottonwood leaned over
the water, its roots bared by spring tides. Here dad would sit…

Sprawled precariously
on a low-lying branch
I'd survey the world
around me.

Stave River, Mission City, BC
Photographer Unknown

The current swiftly pulled
brown water and
    Whirlpools swirled
grasping
at each twig and branch.

The sky so blue
I could look and look
    and lose myself
in its panorama of glory.

The mountain jutted
darkly behind us
    The train
screamed its warning
as it followed the curves
where the mountain met the river.

It rumbled past
then slowly faded
    in the distance.

War once more!
The land of his birth
battered by bombing
and fighting to survive.
He'd listen to the news
with a heavy heart
    then silently hoe the garden.

At thirteen, I was in the hospital again. Mom and
dad came to see me once a month. I felt kinship with
those having disfiguring disabilities. We accepted
and helped each other, and no one ever teased.

Pearl Harbour
    rumours of submarines
enemies at our shore.

Japanese fishermen
viewed with suspicion.
All they had was taken
    houses, lands, cars
    all gone.
They were moved inland
with nothing
but a suitcase.

Home again, I would find Dad in the garden. I'd look for him after school, and seeing him, I'd cry. I knew he would die young. *Oh God, how could I ever live without him?*

Daddy rested more often now. We would sit in the evenings, leaning back against a weeping willow tree, which dripped its branches around about us.

We were silent
kindred souls
   absorbed
in wordless conversation
of the wonder of creation
around us.

Dad in the Garden
Collection of Family Photographs

One step at a time, my little grey-haired daddy plodded.
Hands and feet worked in monotonous rhythm in the battle
against the ever-growing weeds. He bent low over the earth.

"Just call me the old sod-buster," he jested lightly.

He leaned heavier upon his hoe, as though the
very earth was calling back its own. He would
lift his eyes to survey the hills around.

Great sadness filled my being as, each day, I would
hurry home from school to find him. His quiet love
was a balm to my crying soul. He seemed to shrink
before my eyes, and I was filled with fear for him.

He spent his years as a tale that is told. He
died as he lived, with thoughts for others.

"Don't worry about me."

"From dust thou art and unto dust thou shalt return."

The shovelful of dirt rattled over the casket. The breath of
life had been removed from this figure formed from dust.

Later in the evening
I walked
through the hollow house.
His favourite chair
still bore the imprint
   of his body
his coat
still hung upon its hook.
The house was full of him
   but he was
not.

I rushed into the garden, the fruit of his labour. The
peas hung heavy on the vine. Carrots showed bright
orange at their base. All around, his garden burst with
energy in living colour. But he was not...

"Where are you Daddy?"
My tears mingled
with the black dirt
beneath my knees.
Only the empty wind
brushed
my wet cheeks
in silence.

"Are you there, God?
Do you hear my cry,
    or do I call to the wind
in vain?

What will I do, God?"

Home was home no more. We had been
held together by unseen cords of love. Without
Dad, we would each walk a lonely road.

Hilda Sanders
Collection of Family Photographs

When I was nineteen, I moved to the city and got a job
on an assembly line, putting together toasters and irons,
adding our piece and passing it on from hand to hand.

B.C. Electric Rly Co – Observation Car – Teddy Lyons Conductor, Granville Street,
Vancouver
Credits: Photographer – Harry Bullen

Vancouver Engineering Works
Credits: "The City of Vancouver Archives" Reference Code: AM54-S4-:BUP491
Major Matthews Collection

We laughed and joked and became friends. I worked
hard, for I had something to prove. My legs ached
with fatigue. If people showed pity in their eyes, I
ignored it, worked harder, and smiled more.

Many people
    so alone;
busy people
overloaded with parcels.
Tired old men
with lunch buckets
    their stories
etched
in lines
upon their faces.

Granville Street, Vancouver, B.C.
Credits: "The City of Vancouver Archives" Reference Code: AM1545-S3-1223
Photographers: Coltman, Don
Steffens, Colmer

Each of us is as a lonely island
that cannot reach the other.

"Come to me
   all you who labour
and I will give you rest."

An emptiness within longed for that rest
but I could not
   I would not
"Later, Lord, but not now!"

My heart cried for little things
like babies to feed
   care for
and watch
them grow.

For the tenderness
of a husband's love
and to be a mother
   to cuddle
and be cuddled.

Was it to be
only a daydream
unfulfilled?

Wonder of wonders! I met my man, and we were
married. To me, Del was a man among men. Most of all, he
treated me as if I were totally normal, and that I became.

Hilda and Del
Collection of Family Photographs

No dreamer this
   my husband
but a doer of deeds.

A man who fished
   for fish
not idly contemplating
mirages
on sky and water.

I loved the very
strength of him.

The shelter he provided
for my soul
   to sally forth
in dreams
always to return
to its safe
   haven.

Hilda and Del, Wedding, 1948
Photographer Unknown

No one knew of my silent worry before the birth of my first child, but she was a rosebud of perfection.

I ran my fingers over her button nose
    dainty mouth
eyes fringed with fragile lashes.
She had a perfect body.

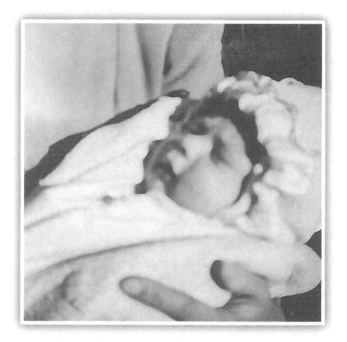

Linda
Collection of Family Photographs

"Oh God
    whose fingers formed the heavens
and earth
    who measured the waters
in the hollow of your hand…
thank you!"

"I wouldn't go there!" warned the shipping clerk. "Nothing there but bush and mosquitos!"

Mr. Webb, our landlord, gave us a fatherly hug. "Wish you wouldn't leave!"

He shook his head sadly. My mom said nothing at all, for even though she dearly loved two-year-old Linda, she knew we'd made up our minds.

Linda with my mom, Emma Sanders
Collection of Family Photographs

In the early fifties
we headed north
    past mounds of hay
forked into piles.
Cows lifting heads
near hip-roofed barns
    mostly red.
The only place
I'd ever known
    but I was leaving
to follow the river
to places new.

The mountains closed in on both sides. We turned
a corner and gone was my beautiful valley.

Our car
growled over gravel
as we travelled
ever onward
    and upward.
Trees clung to rocky heights
    standing defiant
misshapen by the wind and rain.
Yellow blooms
tucked in crevasses
in rocks
    stark and bare.

We snaked our way higher. Our car seemed to drop off into space as the thin ribbon of road twisted to dizzying heights. I stifled a gasp and closed my eyes. Del crawled to a stop.

"Better wait for that car!"

Tunnel in the Fraser Canyon
Collection of Family Photographs

Fraser Canyon
Credits: "The City of Vancouver Archives"
Reference Code: AM1545-S3-:CVA586-3029
Photographers: Coltman, Don Steffens, Colmer

Credits: "The City of Vancouver Archives"
Reference Code: AM1477-1S5-:CVA 1477-264.18
Photographer: Taylor, Louis Denison

From the lip of the road
I looked down
   to the river
churning over rocks
   far below.
Gravel from our tires
rolled down
the deep abyss.

We corkscrewed downward to the river then, once
again, climbed toward the summit. We pulled over and
stopped whenever a southbound car approached. We
drove the goat trail pushed through by prospectors.

Fraser Canyon
Credit: "The City of Vancouver Archives"
Reference Code: AM54-S4-2-:CVA371-2919
Photographer: Moore, W.J

Shadows lengthened
   darkness came softly
the canyon
behind us
sage brush and desert
ahead
   the protecting arms
of a pine tree
seemed like
a good place
   to stop.

Del took a blanket and pillow, stretching out on
the front seat. The foot well in the back seat was
full of boxes, making a perfect bed for Linda and
me. We got cosy under blankets and slept.

Daylight
filtered through branches
as on we went
    following the river.

Cars travelling ahead
covered all
with a blanket
of dust.

We passed
irrigated fields
and barren deserts
as we twisted
our way
    northward.

Train along the Fraser River
Collection of Family Photographs

At the end of the day, we passed over a railway
bridge across the Fraser River at Prince George.

I stared longingly
at the muddy water
that would flow by
my childhood home.

The next morning, we turned west. The road
became a trail corduroying over swamps...

meandering
past farms
hills and valleys
and trees.

We travelled
onward
to Burns Lake
    boardwalks
mud for streets
rough and tough.

I surveyed it all
and wished for home
but here we were
    and we were here
to stay!

Burns Lake, BC
Credits: Prince Rupert City & Regional Archives & Museum of Northern B.C.,
Wrathall Collection, WP995-25-4567
Burns Lake, B.C. 1948
Negative number: JRW559G

Del bought a small sawmill on a section of land
with a handshake and a promise to pay as he sold
lumber. Both men honoured their commitment.

Life seemed harsh and stripped down to bare necessities.
I felt the lack of modern conveniences keenly.

Our Lumber Truck
Collection of Family Photographs

All things were obtained by battling the very elements.
But each victory tasted sweet as battles were won.
There was a challenge to life, and I rose to meet it.

A time to bake
    a time to scrub
a time to learn
    to light a lamp.

Peeling Ties
Collection of Family Photographs

I eyed the gas lamp nervously. The room seemed smaller in the gathering gloom. Through the window, the sky showed dull slate. Spruce and Jack pine crowded close like menacing giants around the cabin. A rutted road made a narrow opening through the trees. An owl hooted, and in the distance, another answered hauntingly. I shivered convulsively and returned to my contemplation of the lamp. It sat upon the table beneath the window. I reached down and shook it. The gas inside sloshed vacantly announcing that it was nearly empty. I walked to the door and stepped out into the dusk, hastening to a nearby shed. I groped in the windowless darkness until my hand touched the metal of the gas can.

I hurried back to the cabin. Picking up the funnel from the shelf by the door, I once again faced the hated lamp. I poured with shaky hands. Cold gas trickled down my arm and dripped from my elbow onto the rough wooden floor. Opening the valve, I gingerly struck a match close to the mantle of the lamp. The sudden burst of flames glowed red. It changed into white brightness, chasing shadows back into the corners of the room.

The dull roar of a heavily loaded truck was faintly heard. I quickly set the table then checked the stew simmering on the back of the wood stove. The lamp glowed invitingly. I sat watching through the window within its circle of light. Headlights stabbed the blackness between the trees. The motor stopped, and heavy footsteps were heard. He slumped on the chair beside the door wearily removing his boots.

"I had trouble, sorry I'm late."

The never-ending seasons systematically scrawled their imprints on the pages of time…

Spring was mud and mosquitoes,
the sweet song of the chickadee
a trout tugging on the line.

Summer was a busy time
packing slabs, peeling ties
    making meals
a few stolen hours spent by the lake
Each moment savoured
    too soon gone.

Frosty mornings
heralded the fall
    the waning warmth of afternoons
soon dwindled.
The autumn moon
illuminated silent trees
with its silver splendour.

All was overtaken
    by winter
which held me within its tight cloak
of waist-deep snow.
Cold crept into my bones.
My legs would ache
    like a tooth with a rotten core.
Pain restricted my movements
and put an edge to my voice.

I grew up into the real life
of living in the bush
    scrubbing clothes
packing water, chopping wood
keeping the wood fire heated.

Going fishing
Del almost always
catching one or two Char;
we'd eat them
    smoke them

give them away.

I began to enjoy bush life
    down-to-earth people
Mrs Del the natives called me.

Wheels groaned over gravel
then jarred to a stop.
Swaybacked horses
    dropped their heads
to feed.
Billy goat smells
permeated the house.

"Hallo Missus!"
    laughter crackled loudly.
Voluptuous pockets
produced penny candy.
I pushed the kettle
to the heat of the stove
    and settled back
to listen to incredible tales
happily told
by the old-timers.

Here we had more children. I had two miscarriages, and
Del—with tears—buried our two little boys out back among
the trees. Soon after, three more children were born to us.

Del with Linda, Cliff and Randy
Collection of Family Photographs

"Thank you, God
  for these my children
all so very loved by me."

Linda and Cindy
Collection of Family Photographs

A few years later, prices of lumber went down.
Timber was harder to get, so when Del had an oppor-
tunity to buy a welding shop, he took it. After a day
of instruction, he was ready for business. It came in
slowly, mostly charged—and often not paid.

We sold our lumber truck
   then our tractor
to live.

Getting desperate
I opened a café close by
    baking pies each morning
chopping wood
    for the cookstove
carrying buckets of water
    from the lake
going next door
for groceries daily
    as I had no fridge
and no time for my little ones
who played at my feet
    going outside
through the open door

"She was in the middle of the road!"
The truck driver carried
my two year old
    Cindy
under his arm
like a sack of potatoes.
"Just about hit her!" he accused.

Too busy
    I cried
"But we need to eat!"
A gentle voice tugged at me

    "Come, my child
I will lead you!"

Too busy
   my heart cried.

One evening, Del took the children home for bed.
Four-year-old Randy had been playing with Jackie, my
friend Nettie's son. When Randy went home, Jackie
found another playmate. They were peddling their
tricycles on the wharf—the ferry having left to cross
the lake. Up and over, Jackie went into the water.

I heard Nettie's scream:
"My baby's drowning
   my baby's drowning!"
We all came running.

The lake was clear as glass
   but Jackie clung to the weeds
on the lake bottom.

The ferry came back
   churning up water and
Jackie came up
   white
and still.

Gripping the rail of the wharf
   I watched
as they breathed air into Jackie
not wanting
to give up.

*"Oh God, make him
breathe!"*
I plead.
Our neighbour
    Harvey
was standing
silently by.

Knowing that he was a Godly man,
    I asked
"Doesn't it say if two
    or three
agree
it shall be done?"

My question startled him
but he had
    no answer.

The ferry
brought a doctor
    he listened for a heartbeat
then sadly
shook his head.

He lay
　　as though asleep
stark reality of death

Nettie wrung her hands
　　twisting hand on hand
hand on hand
mutely showed forth
the anguish
　　of her soul.

We sat together
all night
holding hands
　　silently
with tears streaming
down our faces
　　no words could
comfort.

The next day, I closed the café and walked away, then
spent hours sitting with my children by the lake. I sat
oblivious to the cold winds that blew from off the water.
I almost welcomed the pain in my legs as the cold seeped
through my clothes. It was a relief from the pain in my soul.

Francois Lake Ferry
Credits: Prince Rupert City & Regional Archives & Museum of Northern B.C.,
Wrathall Collection, WP995-25-4567."
Francois Lake, B.C.
Negative number: JRW330A

Will one of mine be next?

Is there a God who masterminds it all and balances,
within His hand, this earthly ball?

Idle hand sifts sand
over idle hand
and there
     between my fingers
an agate caught
   whose opal centre
gleams
     glistening in the sun.

Beside the lulling, lapping lake
I sit and stare
at a great expanse
    of sky and water
and i made small in size
awed by the glories in the girth of it
    another pebble on the shore.
Little things are there to glean
    like driftwood...

What perilous journey
brought you here
    upon my mantle?
Were you a limb or tree
    uprooted from life
which tore you
    breaking you
as you were dashed
into the water?

I picked you from the rubble
    on the shores of a quiet bay
amid the tumbled mass
thrown high upon the beach
your edges knocked off
by the flaying waves
    which pushed you
relentlessly toward the unmovable rocks
    that battered and broke you.

Now you sit gnarled driftwood
warm lines of brown
show through
your whitened surface.
    I have lovingly buffed you
and polished you
until you gleam.

So life must be strained
lest all be naught
    and the last
great pearl of life
remain unfound
    and life at its end
be void and vacant ground.

A billowy cloud momentarily crossed in front of
the sun as though an unseen hand guided its path
across the sky. Its shadow fell upon the water, revealing
the darkness in its depth. A frightening unknown
chilled me where I sat—suspended between sky and
water—held only by the splintered boards beneath.

Randy
Collection of Family Photographs

I remembered my dad more often now and won-
dered at his great love. My mind teemed with words.
I left my work undone as I let these memories pour
themselves upon the page. I had only to close my eyes
and there were my young days—and always Daddy.

He was a little man, content to do the little things.
Why was he able to do menial tasks humbly, and
not ask more? The answer was not found upon
the page. I wept as I left the story unfinished.

Spring finally arrived. The snow was gone, and the grass was beginning to turn green. Harvey stood at our door, hat in hand, awkwardly shuffling his feet.

"Would you like to come with us for Easter service?" he asked.

And so we went. Arriving at the community hall, we were greeted by crowds gathering for the service. Although the room was full, we were ushered to seats near the front. A hush fell over the crowd as a lady began to sing. A thrill rippled through me. It was as though a message in song was sent from the throne of God, just for me...

There's not a friend like the lowly Jesus.
No, not one! No, not one!
None else could heal all our soul's diseases,
No, not one! No, not one!

I drank in the words...

Jesus knows all about our struggles,
He will guide till the day is done;
There's not a friend like the lowly Jesus.
No, not one! No, not one!

"Oh yes, Lord," my longing heart cried...

There's not an hour that He is not near us
No night so dark, but His love can cheer us

(No, Not One! Johnson Oatman, 1895)

I sat transfixed, letting go, knowing my life would never be the same. The preacher rose to speak ...

"He was sold for the price of a slave ...
  He reigned in glory ...
wore a crown of thorns.
  Cruel hands pierced His hands and feet ..."
Then he said,
"He died for you.
  Will you live
for Him?"

The eyes of my understanding were opened.
I saw Him hanging on the cross ...
  how large a love
  that held Him there
    for me

Finally spent I gave my life to Him.

"... as an hiding place from the wind, and a covert
from the tempest; as rivers of water in a dry place, as the
shadow of a great rock in a weary land. Isaiah 32:2, KJV

"Thank you, Lord
for the path of pain
  the sighing soul
that brought me here to You."

The eternal lover
    of my soul
flooded my lonely island
    with His love
and gave me
a song in my night.

I have a song to sing
    though in a strange land
I have a house
    not made with mortal hands

eternal in the heavens.

Now 86 years old, Hilda lives with her husband Del, at Heritage Manor in Fort St. John, British Columbia.

Her faith remains steadfast and strong in the face of many difficulties and changes.

Hilda's Family
From left to right: Randy, Rachel, Cindy, Matthew,
Hilda, Clifford, Linda, Del. (Late 1960's)

"... But now, O Lord, thou art our father;
we are the clay, and thou our potter;
and we are all the work of thy hand.
Isaiah 64:8 KJV

Printed in Canada